Ekadashi Vrat

By Divinebharat

ISBN: 978-93-5525-607-2

Publisher: Divinebharat
www.divinebharat.co

Preface

(Meaning: The Eleventh Lunar Day)

According to the Vedic lunar calendar, Ekadashi falls twice every month — once during the waxing phase (Shukla Paksha) and once during the waning phase (Krishna Paksha) of the Moon. This fast is considered especially sacred in the Vaishnava tradition. On this day, devotees worship Lord Vishnu and observe fasting, partial fasting, or fruit-based diets to exercise control over their senses.

The purpose of this observance is not merely to wash away sins, but to cultivate self-restraint, spiritual discipline, and inner growth. Hence, Ekadashi is regarded as a great vow that purifies life and brings balance and discipline to the mind and body.

Many devotees recite the Vishnu Sahasranāma on Ekadashi as an act of devotion. In many temples, this sacred hymn is chanted collectively on special Ekadashis. This tradition represents both authenticity and devotional sincerity, harmonizing with scriptural ideals.

On this holy day, devotees remember, chant, and meditate upon the Divine.

This book also presents the story of the origin of Ekadashi Devi, which is associated with Lord Vishnu, along with the Ārati (prayer) of Ekadashi Mata and Lord Vishnu.

Senses to Be Restrained on Ekadashi

Five Sense Organs (Jñānendriyas):

1. Eyes (Netra) – Avoid impure or unnecessary sights; keep your vision pure and focused on the divine.
2. Ears (Karna) – Refrain from hearing impure or negative speech; listen only to sacred words, stories, and hymns.
3. Nose (Ghrāṇa) – Stay away from unpleasant or distracting odors; embrace purity and fragrance in your surroundings.
4. Skin (Tvachā) – Avoid indulgence in sensual contact; accept only soothing and sacred touch.
5. Tongue (Rasanā/Jihvā) – Refrain from craving tastes; take only fruits or permitted fasting foods while chanting the Divine Name.

Five Organs of Action (Karmendriyas):

1. Hands (Hasta) – Avoid impure deeds; engage in worship, prayer, charity, and virtuous acts.
2. Feet (Pāda) – Do not visit unholy places or bad company; walk only to temples, gatherings, and sacred spaces.
3. Speech (Vāk) – Abstain from lies, gossip, or harsh words; speak truthfully, gently, and with remembrance of the Divine.
4. Genitals (Upastha) – Maintain self-control and observe celibacy.
5. Excretory Organ (Pāyu) – Follow cleanliness, purity, and discipline in daily conduct.

Inner Instrument (Antaḥkaraṇa):

- Mind (Manaḥ) – The ruler of the senses. The true aim of the Ekadashi fast is to withdraw the mind from worldly distractions and fix it in devotion to the Divine. Thus, Ekadashi is not merely abstaining from food but practicing control of the mind and senses, enabling the devotee to rise above sin and receive divine grace.

The Diet of Ekadashi

The observance of the Ekadashi fast can be practiced in several ways. A devotee may choose the form of fasting that suits their health, lifestyle, and spiritual goal. It is not merely about abstaining from food but about practicing discipline and devotion toward the Divine.

1. Nirjala (Without Water):

The devotee abstains completely from food and even water for the entire day. This is considered the most austere and highest form of fasting.

2. Jalāhāra (Water Only):

Only water is consumed throughout the day; no other food is taken.

3. Kṣīrabhogī (Milk Diet):

The devotee partakes only of milk and milk-based items.

4. Phalāhāra (Fruits Only):

Only fruits and natural foods such as seasonal fruits are consumed.

5. Naktabhogī (Evening Meal):

The devotee fasts through the day and eats once after sunset. The food includes fasting-appropriate ingredients such as sabudana (sago), singhara (water chestnut), sweet potato, potato, and peanuts.

Note: Grains (like rice, wheat, barley, millet) and pulses/legumes (like arhar, moong, chana) are avoided on Ekadashi.

Thus, the Ekadashi fast can be observed at different levels — from the rigorous nirjala fast to the simpler phalāhāra or naktabhoga. The core purpose remains the same — to restrain the senses and dedicate the day entirely to devotion and remembrance of the Divine.

Ekadashi List

No	Ekadashi Name	Month / Paksha	Significance	Dietary Rules
1	Utpanna Ekadashi	Margashirsha Krishna	Brings success in all pious deeds	Fruits only
2	Mokshada Ekadashi	Margashirsha Shukla	Grants liberation and destroys sins	Fruits or milk
3	Saphala Ekadashi	Pausha Krishna	Brings prosperity and salvation	Fruits, milk
4	Pausha Putrada Ekadashi	Pausha Shukla	Grants progeny and well-being	No grains; fruits & milk
5	Shattila (Tilda) Ekadashi	Magha Krishna	Bestows merit of charity; removes sins	Sesame, fruits, milk
6	Jaya Ekadashi	Magha Shukla	Removes ghostly afflictions and evil influences	No grains; fruits only
7	Vijaya Ekadashi	Phalguna Krishna	Removes obstacles; brings victory and success	Fruits, milk, water

8	Amalaki Ekadashi	Phalguna Shukla	Grants virtue, purity, and good health	Amla (Indian gooseberry)
9	Papamochani Ekadashi	Chaitra Krishna	Destroys all sins and impurities	Fruits only
10	Kamada Ekadashi	Chaitra Shukla	Grants offspring and fulfills desires	Fruits, milk
11	Varuthini Ekadashi	Vaishakha Krishna	Brings wealth, fortune, and protection	Fruits only
12	Mohini Ekadashi	Vaishakha Shukla	Removes illusion and worldly attachment	Fruits, milk
13	Apara Ekadashi	Jyeshtha Krishna	Frees from all sins and gives purity	No grains; fruits allowed
14	Nirjala Ekadashi	Jyeshtha Shukla	Supreme fast; gives result of all Ekadashis	Complete fast, no water
15	Yogini Ekadashi	Ashadha Krishna	Cures diseases and grants good health	Fruits, milk
16	Devshayani Ekadashi	Ashadha Shukla	Marks beginning of Chaturmas period	Fruits only

17	Kamika Ekadashi	Shravana Krishna	Best for worshipping Lord Vishnu	Fruits, milk
18	Shravana Putrada Ekadashi	Shravana Shukla	Brings purity and spiritual upliftment	Fruits only
19	Aja Ekadashi	Bhadrapa da Krishna	Destroys all sins and past karmas	Fruits, milk
20	Parivartini (Parshva) Ekadashi	Bhadrapa da Shukla	Lord Vishnu turns in His divine sleep	Fruits only
21	Indira Ekadashi	Ashwin Krishna	Grants peace to ancestors (Pitru Moksha)	Fruits, water
22	Padmini Ekadashi	Adhika Masa Shukla	Brings immense virtue and blessings	Fruits only
23	Rama Ekadashi	Ashwin Shukla	Grants liberation and happiness	Fruits only
24	Parama Ekadashi	Adhika Masa Kartika Krishna	Brings fortune, virtue, and prosperity	Fruits only
25	Prabodhini (Dev Uthani) Ekadashi	Kartika Shukla	Marks end of Chaturmas; Vishnu awakening day	Fruits only

Ekadashi Utpatti Ki Katha

Ek samay ki baat hai – jab 88,000 mahaan rishigan, jinmein Shaunak aadi pramukh the, Naimisharanya mein ekatrit hue. Sabhi maharshiyon ne param puranavid, brahmagyani Shri Sootji Maharaj se nivedan kiya –
"Hey Sootji! Aap sarvagya hain, kripya humein Ekadashi vrat ki utpatti tatha uske mahatmya ke vishay mein vistaar se batayiye."

Rishiyon ke is prashn ko sunkar Sootji ne kaha –
"Hey mahaan tapasviyon! Yahi prashn Mahabharat kaal mein Dharmaraj Yudhishthir ne bhi Bhagwan Shri Krishna se unke pancham Ashwamedh yagya ke avsar par kiya tha. Us samay Shri Krishna ne Ekadashi ke mahatmya ki jo katha

sunai thi, wahi main aap sabko sunata hoon, dhyanpurvak shravan kijiye."

Bhagwan Shri Krishna ne kaha – "Ek varsh mein baarah maas hote hain aur pratyek maas mein do Ekadashiyan aati hain. Is prakar poore varsh mein kul 24 Ekadashiyan hoti hain. Jab Adhimas (adhik maas) aata hai, tab usmein bhi do Ekadashiyan hoti hain. Is prakar kul milakar 26 Ekadashiyan hoti hain. Inke naam is prakar hain –

1. Utpanna Ekadashi
2. Mokshada Ekadashi
3. Saphala Ekadashi
4. Paush Putrada Ekadashi
5. Shattila Ekadashi
6. Jaya Ekadashi
7. Vijay Ekadashi

8. Amalaki Ekadashi
9. Papamochini Ekadashi
10. Kamada Ekadashi
11. Varuthini Ekadashi
12. Mohini Ekadashi
13. Apara Ekadashi
14. Nirjala Ekadashi
15. Yogini Ekadashi
16. Devshayani Ekadashi
17. Kamika Ekadashi
18. Shravan Putrada Ekadashi
19. Aja Ekadashi
20. Parivartini Ekadashi
21. Indira Ekadashi
22. Papankusha Ekadashi
23. Rama Ekadashi
24. Prabodhini Ekadashi (Devuthani)

Adhimas ki donon Ekadashiyan –

1. Padmini Ekadashi
2. Parama Ekadashi

Bhagwan Shri Krishna ne aage kaha – "In sabhi Ekadashiyon ka phal unke namaanusar hi prapt hota hai. Jo bhi shraddha aur niyampurvak in vraton ka paalan karta hai, use dharma, artha, kaam aur moksha – chaaron purusharth sahaj hi mil jaate hain."

Satyug mein ek Mur naamak daitya hua jo atyant parakrami tha. Usne Indra, Surya, Vasu, Brahma, Vayu, Agni sabhi devtaon ko parajit kar diya. Bhaybheet devta Bhagwan Vishnu ki sharan mein gaye. Bhagwan ne devtaon ke saath uspar aakraman kiya. Sahasron varsh tak yudh chalta raha. Antatah Bhagwan ek gufa mein vishram karne lage. Daitya Mur wahan pahucha aur soye hue Bhagwan ko maarne ka vichar karne laga. Tabhi Bhagwan Vishnu ke shareer se ek tejsvini kanya prakat hui. Us kanyaa ne Mur se bhishan yudh kiya aur uske sabhi astr-shastr nash kar diye. Ant mein usne talvaar se Mur ka sir kaat diya.

Jab Bhagwan Vishnu jaage to unhone us kanya ko dekha. Prasann hokar bole — “Vatsay! Maang jo chaho.”

Kanya boli —

“Prabhu! Aaj ke din jo manushya upvaas karenge unhe saare paapon se mukti mile. Jo keval raatri mein bhojan karenge unhe aadha phal, aur jo dopahar mein bhojan karenge unhe uska chauthai phal mile. Parantu jo poorn upvaas karenge ve karodon kalp tak swarg ka bhog kar ant mein aapke dhaam ko prapt hon.”

Bhagwan ne var pradan kiya aur bole

"Aaj se tum Ekadashi naam se prasiddh hogi. Jo koi is din vrat karega, uske paap bhasm ho jaayenge aur vah antatah mere dhaam ko prapt hoga."

Is prakar Ekadashi swayam Bhagwan ki shakti swaroopa hain, aur is din upvaas karne se paap nash hokar bhakti aur moksha ki prapti hoti hai.

II Om Jai Jagdish Hare II

Om Jai Jagdish Hare,
Swami! Jai Jagdish Hare I
Bhakt Jano Ke Sankat,
Kshan Mein Door Kare II
Om Jai Jagdish Hare I

Jo Dhyaave Phal Paave,
Dukh Vinase Man Ka I
Swami Dukh Vinase Man Ka I
Sukh Sampatti Ghar Aave,
Kasht Mite Tan Ka II
Om Jai Jagdish Hare I

Maat-Pita Tum Mere,
Sharan Gahun Main Kiski I
Swami Sharan Gahun Main Kiski I
Tum Bin Aur Na Dooja,
Aas Karun Jiski II
Om Jai Jagdish Hare I

Tum Poorn Paramatma,
Tum Antaryami I

Swami Tum Antaryami I

Parabrahm Parameshwar,
Tum Sabke Swami II

Om Jai Jagdish Hare I

Tum Karuna Ke Saagar,
Tum Palan-Karta I

Swami Tum Palan-Karta I

Main Moorakh Khal Kaami,
Kripa Karo Bharta II

Om Jai Jagdish Hare I

Tum Ho Ek Agochar,
Sabke Pranpati I

Swami Sabke Pranpati I

Kis Vidhi Miloon Dayamay,
Tumko Main Kumati II

Om Jai Jagdish Hare I

Deenbandhu Dukh Harta,
Tum Thakur Mere I
Swami Tum Thakur Mere I
Apne Haath Uthao,
Dwar Pada Tere II
Om Jai Jagdish Hare I
Vishay-Vikaar Mitao,
Paap Haro Deva I
Swami Paap Haro Deva I
Shraddha-Bhakti Badhao,
Santan Ki Seva II
Om Jai Jagdish Hare I
Shri Jagdishji Ki Aarti,
Jo Koi Nar Gave I
Swami Jo Koi Nar Gave I
Kahat Shivanand Swami,
Sukh Sampatti Pave II
Om Jai Jagdish Hare I

II Ekadashi Mata ki Aarti II

Om Jai Ekadashi, Jai Ekadashi,
Jai Ekadashi Mata.
Vishnu pooja vrat ko dharan kar,
shakti mukti paata
Om Jai Ekadashi...
Tere naam ginau devi,
bhakti pradan karni.
Gan gaurav ki deni mata,
shastron mein varni
Om Jai Ekadashi...
Margashirsha ke krishnapaksh ki
Utpanna, Vishwatarni janmi.
Shukla paksh mein hui Mokshada,
Muktidata ban aai
Om Jai Ekadashi...
Paush ke krishnapaksh ki,
Safala naamak hai.
Shuklapaksh mein hoy Putrada,
anand adhik rahai
Om Jai Ekadashi...

Naam Shatatila Magh maas mein,
krishnapaksh aavai.
Shukla paksh mein Jaya,
kahavai, vijay sada paavai
Om Jai Ekadashi...
Vijaya Phagun krishnapaksh mein,
Shukla Aamlaki.
Paapmochani krishnapaksh mein,
Chaitra Mahabali ki
Om Jai Ekadashi...
Chaitra Shukla mein naam Kamada,
dhan dene wali.
Naam Varuthini krishnapaksh mein,
Vaisakh maah wali
Om Jai Ekadashi...
Shukla paksh mein hoy Mohini
Apara Jyeshth krishnapakshi.
Naam Nirjala sab sukh karni,
Shuklapaksh rakhi
Om Jai Ekadashi...
Yogini naam Ashadh mein jaano,
krishnapaksh karni.
Devshayani naam kahayo,

Shuklapaksh dharani
Om Jai Ekadashi...
Kamika Shravan maas mein aavai,
krishnapaksh kahiye.
Shravan Shukla hoy pavitra,
anand se rahiye
Om Jai Ekadashi...
Aja Bhadrapad krishnapaksh ki,
Parivartini Shukla.
Indra Ashchin krishnapaksh mein,
vrat se bhavsagar nikla
Om Jai Ekadashi...
Paapankusha hai Shukla paksh mein,
aap haranhari.
Rama maas Kartik mein aavai,
sukhdayak bhaari
Om Jai Ekadashi...
Devotthani Shuklapaksh ki,
dukhnashak Maiya.
Pavan maas mein karoon vinati,
paar karo naiya
Om Jai Ekadashi...

Parma krishnapaksh mein hoti,
jan mangal karni.
Shukla maas mein hoy Padmini,
dukh daridra harni
Om Jai Ekadashi...
Jo koi aarti Ekadashi ki,
bhakti sahit gaave.
So Jan swarg ka vasa,
nishchay hi paave
Om Jai Ekadashi...

9 789355 256072

Printed at Repro India Ltd.